bxje

BULLDOZERS

Dan Osier

PowerKiDS press™

New York

Published in 2014 by The Rosen Publishing Group, Inc.
29 East 21st Street, New York, NY 10010

First Edition

Editor: Amelie von Zumbusch
Book Design: Andrew Povolny

Library of Congress Cataloging-in-Publication Data

Osier, Dan.
 Bulldozers / by Dan Osier. — First edition.
     pages cm. — (Construction site)
 Includes index.
 ISBN 978-1-4777-2859-8 (library binding) — ISBN 978-1-4777-2952-6 (paperback) —
 ISBN 978-1-4777-3029-4 (6-pack)
 1. Bulldozers—Juvenile literature. I. Title.
 TA725.O85 2014
 629.225—dc23
                                    2013015809

Manufactured in the United States of America

CPSIA Compliance Information: W14PK3: For Further Information contact Rosen Publishing, New York, New York at 1-800-237-9932

Contents

Bulldozers are cool! They move dirt and other things.

Some are used in construction. Others are used in mines or on farms.

Some armies use them. The nickname for an Israeli Army one is a Doobi.

8

They are slow. The fastest ones go just 18 miles per hour (29 km/h).

Bulldozers tend to have **tracks**. These keep bulldozers from sinking into soft soil.

The **blade** is in front. It pushes things.

There are three kinds of blades. They are the S blade, the U blade, and the S-U blade.

Some bulldozers have **rippers**.
They are on the back. They tear
up dirt.

Many companies make bulldozers. Caterpillar makes the most.

21

Have you ever seen a bulldozer?

WORDS TO KNOW

blade   ripper   track

WEBSITES

Due to the changing nature of Internet links, PowerKids Press has developed an online list of websites related to the subject of this book. This site is updated regularly. Please use this link to access the list: www.powerkidslinks.com/cs/dozers/

INDEX

24